# ARMS AND ARMOR

*Written by* Chris Gravett
*Illustrated by* Richard Hook, Chris Rothero,
and Peter Sarson

RSVP

RAINTREE
STECK-VAUGHN
P U B L I S H E R S
The Steck-Vaughn Company

*Austin, Texas*

Editor: Dr. Skipp Tullen
Project Manager: Julie Klaus

Library of Congress Cataloging-in-Publication Data
Gravett, Christopher, 1951–
    Arms and armor / written by Chris Gravett; illustrated by
Richard Hook, Chris Rothero, and Peter Sarson.
       p.   cm. — (Pointers)
    Includes index.
    ISBN 0-8114-6190-4
    1. Weapons — History — Juvenile literature.  2. Armor — History —
Juvenile literature.  [1. Weapons — History.  2. Armor — History.]
I. Hook, Richard, ill.  II. Rothero, Christopher, ill.  III. Sarson, Peter, ill.
IV. Title.
U800.G72   1995
623.4'41'09—dc20                              94-7938
                                                 CIP
                                                 AC

Printed and bound in the United States

1 2 3 4 5 6 7 8 9 0 VH 99 98 97 96 95 94

# Foreword

Humans have fought over possessions or land ever since early humans began to grow crops or keep domestic animals. The earliest weapons were probably rocks, sticks, and animal bones and were used in one of two ways. Some were carried to strike a blow or to cut. Other weapons were made to be thrown or shot at the enemy from a distance.

Later, humans developed specially shaped weapons from stone and flint, and by about 5000 B.C., copper was being used. After this came bronze, then iron, and finally steel, which made the hardest armor and sharpest blades. Many other materials have also been used, such as leather, whalebone, and horn.

Soon, those who had to fight began to protect themselves by carrying shields. Sometimes they also wore body armor. Armorers design armor to give the best possible protection against increasingly powerful weapons. It must not be too heavy or so difficult to wear that a soldier cannot move properly. This constant struggle between attack and defense has continued right up to the present day with each manufacturer trying to produce better equipment than his or her rivals.

# Contents

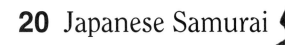

# Early Bronze Weapons

The first soldiers to use bronze were the Sumerians of the ancient Middle East around 3000 B.C. The Sumerians carried spears and large rectangular shields. By about 1400 B.C., Egyptian soldiers, among others, were wearing armor of stiffened fabric and coats covered in small scales. The Assyrians, who rose to power in the Middle East in the late 10th century B.C., were ruthless soldiers. Many wore helmets and body armor, and their horsemen often carried bows and arrows as well. The Assyrian Empire fell around 612 B.C., by which time the Greek city-states were becoming powerful. Greek soldiers wore bronze helmets that covered almost the whole head, and they carried large, round bronze shields. Their spears eventually became 20-foot (6-m) pikes, used in a tight formation called a phalanx.

**3** Lamellar armor was made up of many small pieces of metal, each laced through holes on a leather jacket.

**4** A composite bow was made of several materials, such as wood, horn, and sinew. The archer carried it in a case along with his arrows.

Egyptian soldier of 1800 B.C.

**1** An early form of cloth body armor made of stiffened fabric was worn by this Egyptian soldier. It also protected his shoulders.

**2** This bronze sword, or *khopesh*, shaped like an animal's hind leg, was a typical weapon of the Egyptians. The outer edge was sharpened for cutting and slashing.

Stiff linen groin guard

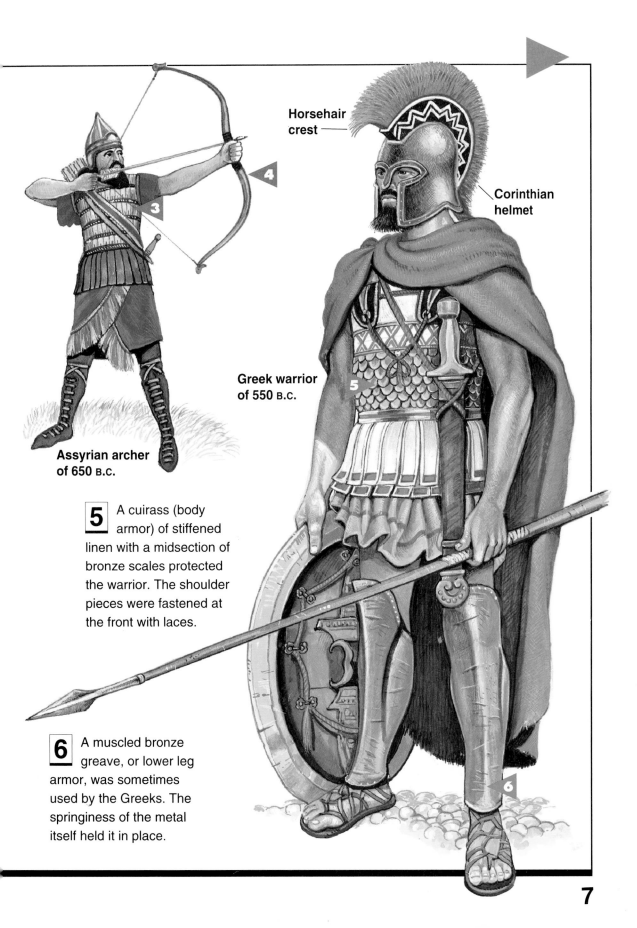

Horsehair
crest

Corinthian
helmet

Greek warrior
of 550 B.C.

Assyrian archer
of 650 B.C.

**5** A cuirass (body
armor) of stiffened
linen with a midsection of
bronze scales protected
the warrior. The shoulder
pieces were fastened at
the front with laces.

**6** A muscled bronze
greave, or lower leg
armor, was sometimes
used by the Greeks. The
springiness of the metal
itself held it in place.

# Chinese Crossbowman

The Chinese had discovered how to cast bronze by 1500 B.C. They made weapons such as the dagger-ax, which had a sharp bronze blade tied firmly to a handle. By 1300 B.C., they were using bronze body armor made of many small plates or one large piece. Around 500 B.C. iron weapons began to appear, but for a long time the metal was of poor quality.

The powerful crossbow was probably invented in the 6th century B.C. It shot an arrow called a bolt. It was far more likely to pierce armor at short range than an arrow fired from the more common bow of the time. Also, it could be held cocked and loaded until the archer wanted to fire.

**3** The armor was made of small bronze plates joined tightly by red laces. Those on the shoulders and stomach had lacing on the outside and moved easily.

**2** The crossbow had a bronze bow attached to a wooden tiller with a groove along the top edge to guide the bolt. The string was drawn back with both hands.

**Chinese crossbowman of 220 B.C.**

**1** The halberd had a spearhead with a second blade that had a beak, or spike, at the back. The blades were made from molten bronze poured into a mold and left to harden.

Bow —

Tiller —

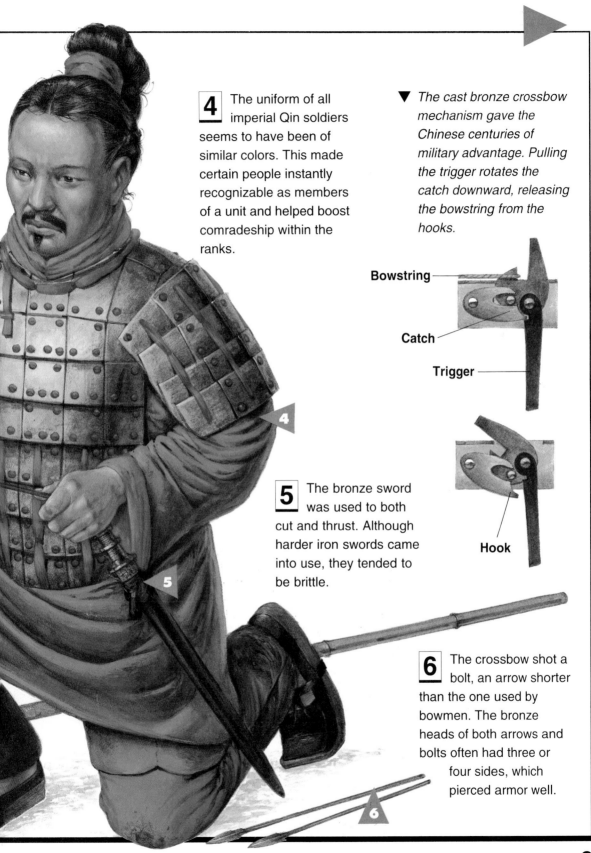

**4** The uniform of all imperial Qin soldiers seems to have been of similar colors. This made certain people instantly recognizable as members of a unit and helped boost comradeship within the ranks.

▼ *The cast bronze crossbow mechanism gave the Chinese centuries of military advantage. Pulling the trigger rotates the catch downward, releasing the bowstring from the hooks.*

Bowstring

Catch

Trigger

**5** The bronze sword was used to both cut and thrust. Although harder iron swords came into use, they tended to be brittle.

Hook

**6** The crossbow shot a bolt, an arrow shorter than the one used by bowmen. The bronze heads of both arrows and bolts often had three or four sides, which pierced armor well.

# ▶ Armies of Iron

In Italy the Romans developed armies that were finally able to defeat the Greeks and break up their phalanxes. After the 2nd century B.C., the Romans gradually conquered much of Europe with disciplined legions of men in armor. Each legion contained several thousand regular troops plus auxiliaries who were not Roman citizens. Legionnaires at first wore mail, made of small metal rings, or a metal plate on the chest. In the 1st century A.D., the *lorica segmentata* came into use. The large shield and tunic were colored to match the soldier's unit. The javelin, or *pilum*, was thrown in a volley by the front ranks before moving in with the short thrusting sword. Cavalrymen and archers often wore mail and sometimes armor made of small scales.

**2** The short iron sword, worn on the right side with a dagger on the left, had a sharp point and was made for thrusting. This was quicker than slashing and did not expose the soldier's body for too long.

**1** The *pilum* had a wooden shaft and an iron head. It dragged down any shield it struck, and as the socket bent on impact, it could not be thrown back.

**Lorica segmentata**

▲
*The lorica was made from iron strips held together by laces, straps, and buckles. These often wore out, so metal fastenings were introduced.*

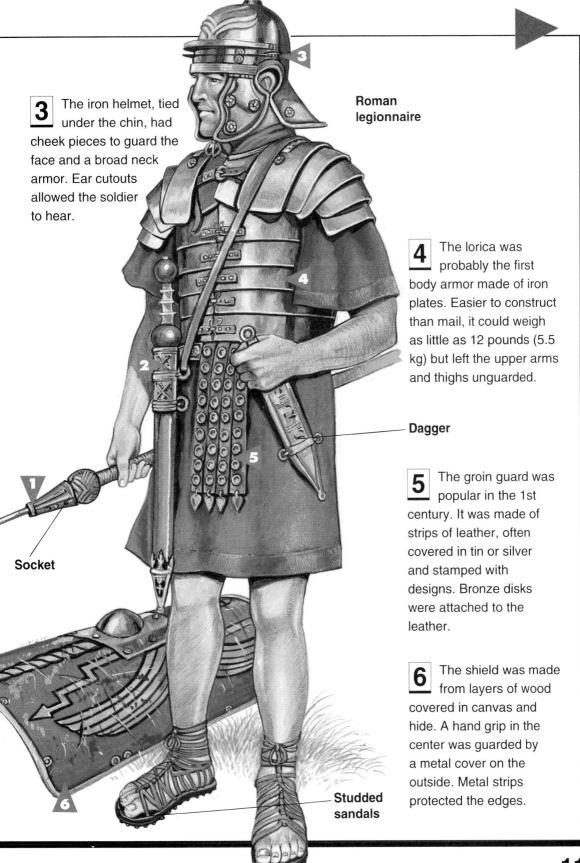

**3** The iron helmet, tied under the chin, had cheek pieces to guard the face and a broad neck armor. Ear cutouts allowed the soldier to hear.

**Roman legionnaire**

**4** The lorica was probably the first body armor made of iron plates. Easier to construct than mail, it could weigh as little as 12 pounds (5.5 kg) but left the upper arms and thighs unguarded.

**Dagger**

**Socket**

**5** The groin guard was popular in the 1st century. It was made of strips of leather, often covered in tin or silver and stamped with designs. Bronze disks were attached to the leather.

**6** The shield was made from layers of wood covered in canvas and hide. A hand grip in the center was guarded by a metal cover on the outside. Metal strips protected the edges.

**Studded sandals**

# The Age of Mail

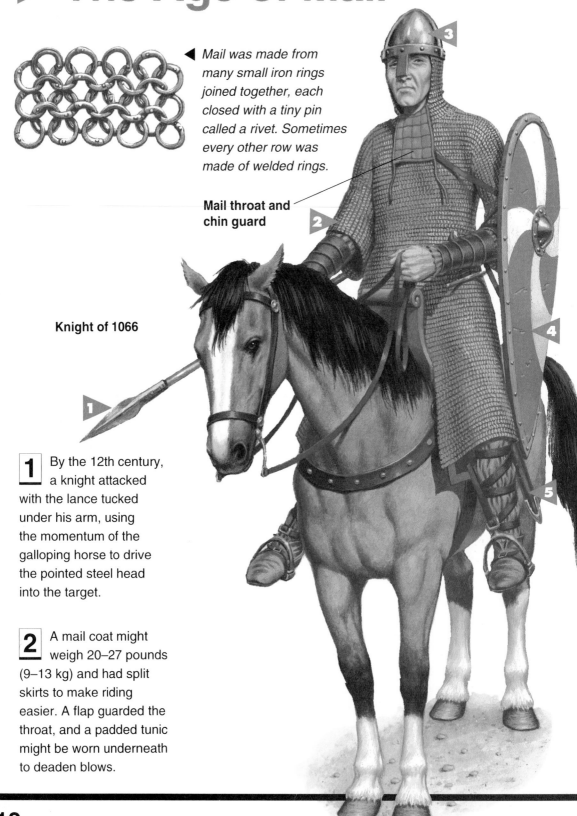

◄ *Mail was made from many small iron rings joined together, each closed with a tiny pin called a rivet. Sometimes every other row was made of welded rings.*

**Mail throat and chin guard**

**Knight of 1066**

**1** By the 12th century, a knight attacked with the lance tucked under his arm, using the momentum of the galloping horse to drive the pointed steel head into the target.

**2** A mail coat might weigh 20–27 pounds (9–13 kg) and had split skirts to make riding easier. A flap guarded the throat, and a padded tunic might be worn underneath to deaden blows.

**3** The steel helmet was shaped to make blows slide off, while the nose guard protected the face from a slashing cut. This type of helmet was used by the knights until the 13th century.

**4** The wooden kite-shaped shield became popular with mounted knights. Unlike the older round shield, it guarded the left side of both horse and rider.

**5** The knight's sword was drawn once the lance had broken. The blade was iron, which made it hard but flexible. It had sharp edges for slashing.

**6** The ax was a popular weapon among the Saxons from Northern Europe and the Viking invaders from Scandinavia. Large axes were swung in both hands to deliver a powerful blow.

Mail continued to be worn by some of the wealthy warriors after the Roman Empire split in A.D. 395. By the 10th century, attacks by raiders, such as the Vikings, had begun. Armored horsemen called knights resisted them. The cost of mail, a sword, and a trained war-horse meant that only wealthy men could be knights. When Norman knights invaded England in 1066, most of them wore long mail coats. From the 12th century, mail often covered the whole body and included stockings of mail. It continued to be worn until the 14th century, by which time better-equipped knights were adding steel plates. Less well-off soldiers continued to use mail until the 17th century.

**Saxon warrior** 6

# ► Eastern Warrior

In Asia and North Africa armor developed differently than in the rest of the world. The cavalrymen were often more lightly armed, and they wore padded coats and lamellar armor. The Mongols, who swept across large areas of Asia in the 13th century, also wore buff leather coats. From the 14th century, mail-and-plate armor was worn, shown here on a 15th-century Turkish horseman. The composite bow, made from layers of wood, horn, and sinew, was often used by archers on horseback. Muslim archers mounted on horseback proved to be a difficult foe for crusaders from Europe, shooting and wheeling away to reload before they could be reached.

**3** The saber was a gently curved single-edged sword used by Eastern horsemen. The shape was said to make it cut better. It was later used by European light cavalry.

**2** The quiver, or arrow case, is covered in decorated cloth. Skilled Turkish archers could shoot accurately from a galloping horse.

**1** This shield is made of cane. Most were circular in shape, and some were decorated. Some iron shields were also used.

◄

*The style of this armor from Tibet, with its lamellar coat and neckguard, may have been taken from armor designed by the Mongols. The helmet pieces are joined by laces.*

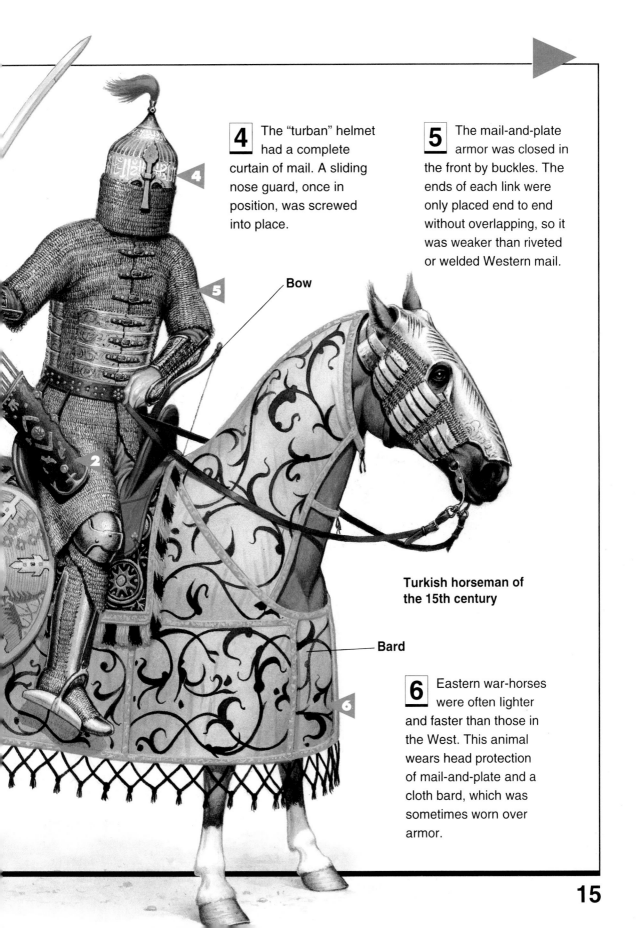

**4** The "turban" helmet had a complete curtain of mail. A sliding nose guard, once in position, was screwed into place.

**5** The mail-and-plate armor was closed in the front by buckles. The ends of each link were only placed end to end without overlapping, so it was weaker than riveted or welded Western mail.

Bow

Turkish horseman of the 15th century

Bard

**6** Eastern war-horses were often lighter and faster than those in the West. This animal wears head protection of mail-and-plate and a cloth bard, which was sometimes worn over armor.

# Medieval Foot Soldiers

Longbows emerged in the 13th century and helped win famous victories for the English in the 14th and 15th centuries. Longbow arrows could penetrate plate armor and so could bolts shot from increasingly powerful crossbows. In Eastern Europe in the 15th century, Hussite rebels used early handguns and cannons, and fought German knights from behind wagon circles. Guns were also used by the Swiss, who used massed formations of men armed with long spears, called pikes, to stop the cavalry. Some infantrymen wore little armor, but others wore pieces of plate or armored jackets over mail.

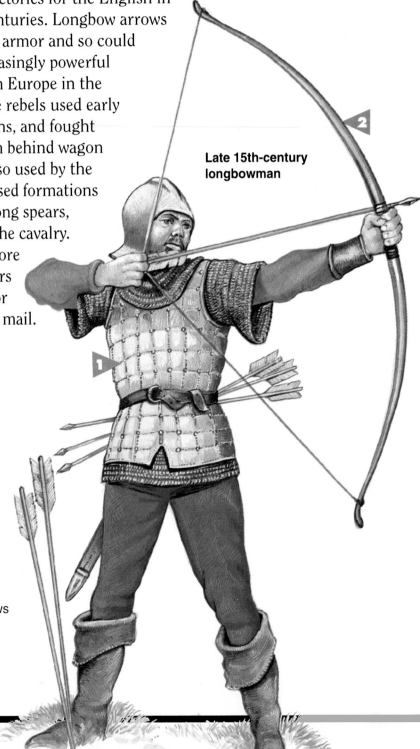

**Late 15th-century longbowman**

**1** The jack was a padded garment stuffed with wool, hair, or similar material and then quilted to keep it in place. Cheap to make, it was surprisingly good at deadening a blow.

**2** The longbow was usually made from yew and was as tall as a man. Constant practice was needed. It shot arrows about 980 feet (300 m), and the arrows could pierce mail at 325 feet (100 m).

**3** This armor made from canvas lined with small pieces of steel is called a brigandine. The rivet heads, which held the steel in place, can be seen on the velvet covering.

**5** The kettle hat had been in use since the 12th century. It let air get to the face, while the brim knocked away missiles.

**Barbute helmet**

**Gunman**

**Crossbowman**

**4** From the 14th century the crossbow might be fitted with a bow that was so powerful, it needed a winch to pull back the string. It was far slower to load than a longbow.

**6** Guns were first used in the 14th century. This 15th-century version is fired by putting a red-hot wire or glowing slow match to a touchhole to ignite the gunpowder inside.

# Steel Plates

Because mail is not rigid, blows can break bones without actually cutting through the rings. More and more steel plates were therefore added, and by 1400, knights were covered from head to foot in plate armor. The pieces could be held together by leather strips attached underneath or by rivets. A rivet on one plate slid in a slot in another plate, or two plates pivoted on a single rivet. Battle armor, like this German example from 1480, weighed about 44 pounds (20 kg). Because the weight was distributed evenly over the body, a man could sit, lie down, run, or mount his horse without help. Plate armor was used until the 17th century.

**1** The mace became popular as plate armor developed. It could both damage the armor and injure the wearer. A sword would often slide off the smooth surface of the armor.

**Laces holding mail gussets**

▲ *The arming doublet worn beneath the armor had pieces of mail to guard unprotected parts and laces to tie the steel plates together.*

**Leather glove riveted inside plates**

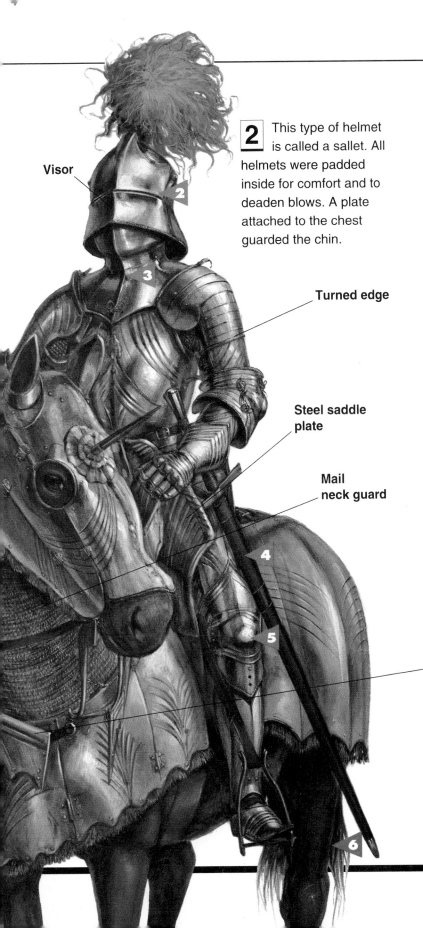

**Visor**

**2** This type of helmet is called a sallet. All helmets were padded inside for comfort and to deaden blows. A plate attached to the chest guarded the chin.

**3** Raised ridges on the steel plates guided weapon points away from the throat and armpits. Turned edges helped to prevent the plates from splitting.

**Turned edge**

**4** Stiff, sharply pointed swords became popular with knights during the 14th century. They could burst mail rings apart, unlike the old cutting swords.

**Steel saddle plate**

**Mail neck guard**

**5** The knee and shin were the first parts of the body to be protected by plates, as a cavalryman's legs were an easy target for foot soldiers. By the 15th century, plates were made for the whole leg.

**Plates to protect reins**

**6** War-horses were strong and nimble, and bred for stamina. Although rich men protected their mounts with armor, the horses were never as well covered as the knights.

# Japanese Samurai

The Japanese warrior class was called the samurai, and its armor was unique. It was made of metal, but because of the damp climate, it was protected by a coat of lacquer to keep it from rusting. The Japanese copied the design of Chinese and Korean lamellar armor in the 5th to 8th centuries but changed it to suit their needs. It was made from strips of small laced plates. There were problems, however. All the lace-holes weakened the metal, the lacing got soaked and filthy, and weapon points could catch in it. So after the 15th century, armor was designed for comfort during the long campaigns and was made of solid strips with far fewer laces. Guns appeared during the period of civil wars (1480–1603), so chest armor was often riveted solidly to resist the impact of musket balls.

**3** On this armor from around 1560, the strips of lacquered metal were held together by threading long silk strips vertically through holes in each plate.

**2** The bow was made from strips of bamboo and other woods that were glued together, lacquered, and bound with rattan. It took a lot of strength to pull a bow like this.

◀ *Twenty-four arrows were carried in a wooden quiver, which was lacquered or covered in fur. A quiver was carried on the right hip. Some quivers completely enclosed the arrows.*

**1** Each shin guard was made of metal strips joined by mail on a cloth backing. A leather patch on the inside stopped it from rubbing against the stirrup when the warrior was on horseback.

**4** The lacquered helmet has the owner's family badge, or *mon*, on the front. Many helmets had large crests, and some face masks had mustaches.

Pheasant feather crest

**5** Arm protection was made of both plates and mail with rings whose ends were butted, or just pushed together. Mail was used more in this period of civil wars.

Decorated rivet heads

**6** The Japanese sword, made of iron and steel, is famous for its single razor-sharp edge. It was often carried blade-upward to give a blow straight from the scabbard. Every samurai also had a short sword.

# Musket and Powder

Full-plate armor became rare after the middle of the 17th century. Better gunpowder meant armor had to be thickened against musket balls and so became uncomfortably heavy. Also, horsemen with lances could not get through foot soldiers armed with 16-foot (4.8-m) pikes. By the 18th century, the pike had been replaced by the bayonet fixed to the end of the musket barrel. Now all the foot soldiers could be armed with a musket.

British redcoats took their massed firepower to America when the colonists fought to gain freedom from British rule in the Revolutionary War. The first shot was fired in April 1775, when 70 American minutemen faced 700 redcoats on the village common at Lexington, Massachusetts.

**1** The ramrod was used to push the musket ball and wad well down into the barrel. Balls and powder were kept in pouches carried by the soldier.

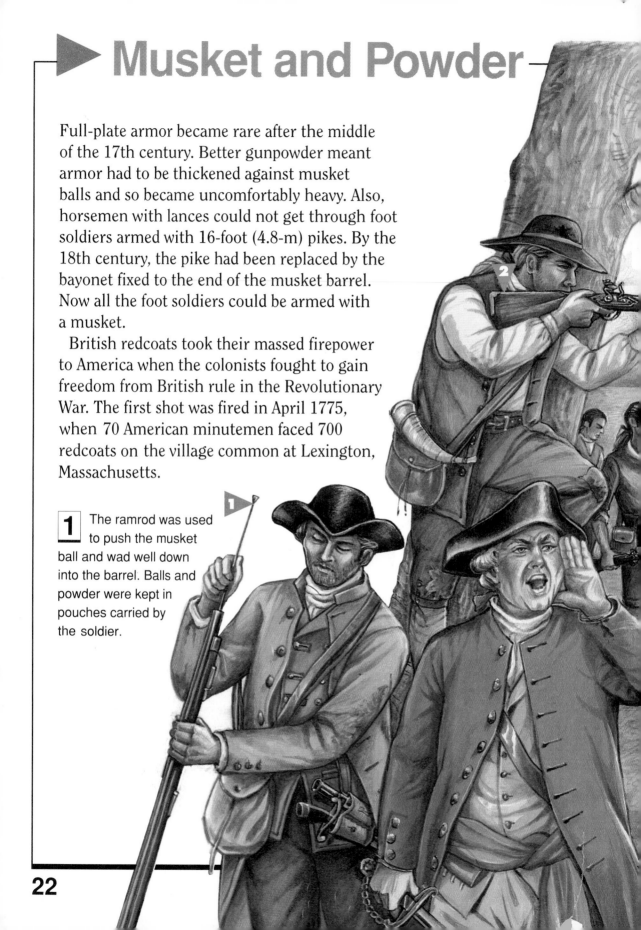

**2** Long-barreled weapons were more likely to hit a target at greater ranges and were used by marksmen to pick off important men, such as officers, and cause confusion in enemy ranks.

**3** The American minutemen were so-called because they could be ready at a minute's notice to fight against the British soldiers.

**4** In contrast to many of the colonists, regular British soldiers wore a uniform to show they formed part of an organized unit.

**5** The British soldiers were drilled to form lines and stand firm under fire, but the American army contained numbers of volunteer farmers and townsmen, called militia, who hid themselves behind trees and fences. This method of warfare proved to be a great advantage to the Americans.

**6** When aiming at a target, the smooth-bore musket was only reliable at a range of about 50 yards (45 m). At greater distances up to about 200 yards (183 m), volley fire from massed ranks was used for maximum effect.

# ► Firearms

**Flint**

**1700s flintlock musket**

**Pan**

**1** The cock held a flint which struck a piece of steel when the musket was fired, sending a shower of sparks to ignite the powder in the pan. This then set off the main charge.

During the Revolutionary War, the flintlock musket was the most popular firearm. By the mid-19th century, most guns had a new firing mechanism called a percussion cap and were reloaded from the breech rather than the muzzle. Later guns stored their cartridges in magazines and were reloaded by operating a sliding bolt. The barrels of these guns were rifled, or cut in spiral grooves, to spin the bullet, giving greater accuracy. American rifles developed from rifles brought to the United States from Europe in the early 1700s.

**1853 carbine**

▼ Early cartridges were torn open, and the powder, ball, and wad rammed down the barrel. Modern metal cartridges are fired either by a hammer striking the rear rim or by a pin striking the rear center.

**1860 repeating rifle**

**Bolt**

**1888 Mauser**

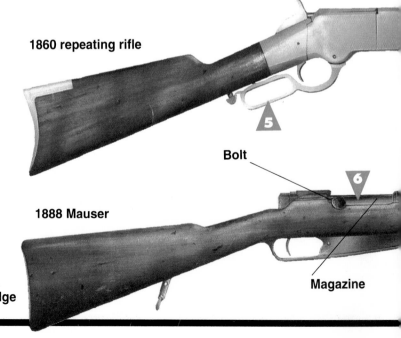

**Magazine**

**Early cartridge**   **Modern cartridge**

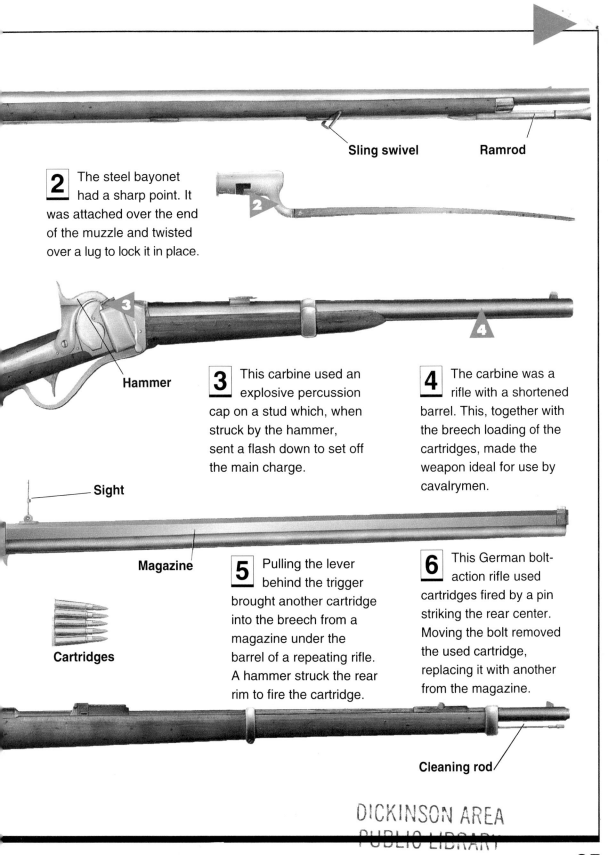

**Sling swivel**

**Ramrod**

**2** The steel bayonet had a sharp point. It was attached over the end of the muzzle and twisted over a lug to lock it in place.

**Hammer**

**3** This carbine used an explosive percussion cap on a stud which, when struck by the hammer, sent a flash down to set off the main charge.

**4** The carbine was a rifle with a shortened barrel. This, together with the breech loading of the cartridges, made the weapon ideal for use by cavalrymen.

**Sight**

**Magazine**

**Cartridges**

**5** Pulling the lever behind the trigger brought another cartridge into the breech from a magazine under the barrel of a repeating rifle. A hammer struck the rear rim to fire the cartridge.

**6** This German bolt-action rifle used cartridges fired by a pin striking the rear center. Moving the bolt removed the used cartridge, replacing it with another from the magazine.

**Cleaning rod**

# ► World Wars

Clip-loaded bolt-action rifles were common in World War I (1914–1918). High-explosive shells and quick-firing heavy machine guns killed many men and put an end to the use of cavalry in battle. Exploding grenades were common. Flame throwers and poison gas were horrifying new weapons. All except gas were used again in World War II (1939–1945), and many soldiers carried submachine guns. Aircraft were making their mark in 1914, and by the 1940s, air crews were wearing armorlike protective clothing.

**2** Steel body armor was worn by German soldiers in World War I when they carried out dangerous tasks close to enemy lines, such as cutting through barbed wire.

**1** Grenades filled with explosives were used in trench warfare. The charge was set off either on impact with the ground or by a short fuse when a pin was pulled.

**3** The gas mask with a filter was used to stop poison gas from being breathed in or getting into the eyes or on the skin of the face.

**1916 German infantryman**

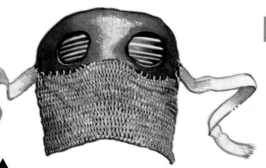

▲

*Shellfire against World War I tanks often tore metal splinters from the inside walls. Crewmen used a mask with a mail curtain to help protect their faces.*

**1944 USAF
waist gunner**

**4** The tin hat worn in both world wars was based on the medieval kettle hat. In World War II foliage was sometimes added to help camouflage the wearer in the undergrowth.

**1942 British
infantryman**

**5** Metal-lined flak jackets and helmets protected some American bomber crews against shrapnel from anti-aircraft and fighter plane fire during World War II.

**6** The British sten gun of World War II was cheap to make but could fire 550 rounds (bullets) per minute. Soldiers put spare clips in the pockets of their uniforms.

# ►Today's Armor

Helmets and vests are often made from a nylon-based material called Kevlar®. Although light to wear, it can stop shrapnel, while ceramic plates are sometimes added to protect against high-powered bullets. One-piece suits protect the body against gas or chemical attack. Assault rifles, which can fire 20 rounds at the flick of a switch, are carried by most troops.

A new range of equipment exists for use by police forces. Helmets and vests are similar to military types, and some body armor can protect against knife thrusts. Rifles that fire rubber bullets or tear gas are sometimes used to break up riots. Armor can even be provided to protect the arms and legs of policemen faced with dangerous dogs.

**2** This single-shot assault rifle can give bursts of fire by flicking a switch. Gas from the explosion removes the used cartridge case and feeds in another round.

**1** Suits for use during chemical warfare have overshoes that seal the pants leg to prevent dangerous materials from getting inside and attacking the skin. Protective gloves are also worn.

**3** The mask and hood completely cover the face. As with all the combat gear, the hood is patterned with camouflage designs to break up the body's outline.

**Modern soldier**

**Desert camouflage**

**Patch of chemical-detecting paper**

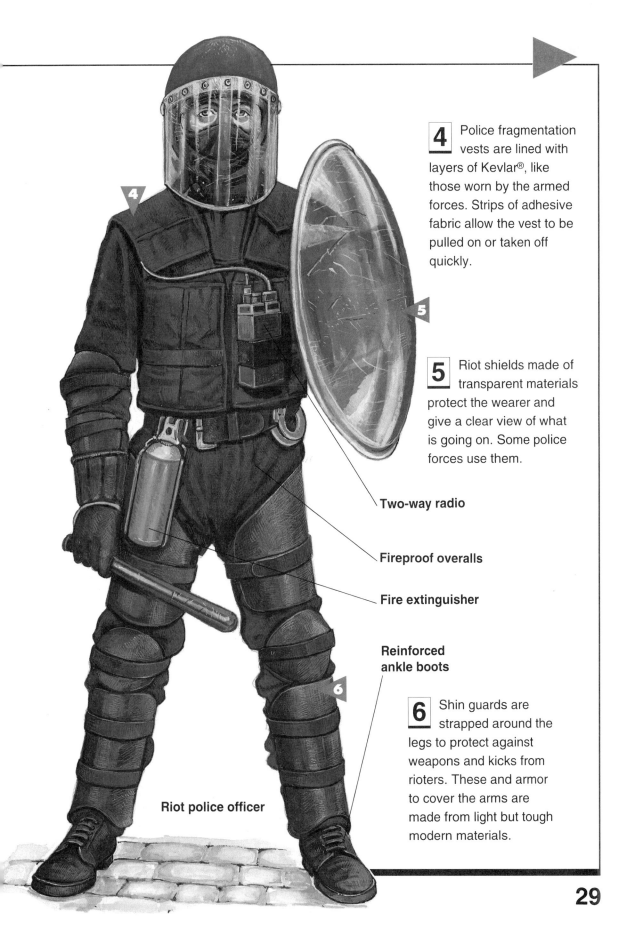

**4** Police fragmentation vests are lined with layers of Kevlar®, like those worn by the armed forces. Strips of adhesive fabric allow the vest to be pulled on or taken off quickly.

**5** Riot shields made of transparent materials protect the wearer and give a clear view of what is going on. Some police forces use them.

Two-way radio

Fireproof overalls

Fire extinguisher

Reinforced ankle boots

**6** Shin guards are strapped around the legs to protect against weapons and kicks from rioters. These and armor to cover the arms are made from light but tough modern materials.

Riot police officer

# Glossary

**Bard**
A protective covering for a horse, usually made of cloth

**Bayonet**
A blade attached to the front of a gun barrel to allow it to be used as a spear

**Breech or chamber**
The part of a gun from which the bullet is fired

**Bronze**
An alloy or mixture of copper and tin

**Buff leather**
A type of untreated leather used with armor. Treated leather contains chemicals that can attack metal.

**Cartridge or round**
The bullet together with its charge of gunpowder. Early forms had a paper covering, while later ones had a metal case.

**Cavalry**
Soldiers on horseback

**Cock**
A pair of metal jaws holding a flint and set on a gun's breech.

When the trigger is pulled, the flint fires a pan of gunpowder.

**Cuirass**
Body armor covering the chest and stomach both front and back

**Doublet**
A close-fitting jacket

**Flak**
Exploding anti-aircraft shells

**Flintlock**
A firearm using a flint to create a spark

**Fragmentation vest**
A garment designed to resist flying fragments of shrapnel

**Fuse**
A connecting cord used to set off an explosive charge

**Gauntlet**
A glove worn with armor to protect the hand

**Greave**
Lower leg armor

**Gusset**
A piece of armor covering the joints in a suit of armor

**Halberd**
A battle-ax and pike mounted on a long handle

**Infantry**
Soldiers on foot

**Lamellar**
Made of many small plates pierced with holes for lacing the plates together

**Lug**
A projection from an object used to attach it to something else

**Mace**
A heavy spiked staff or club

**Machine gun**
A heavy gun that fires shells from a belt in one continuous burst. It is operated by a team of soldiers.

**Magazine or clip**
A container holding a number of cartridges. It is either clipped to the gun or is already attached, in which case the cartridges are fed into it from a holder.

**Mail**
Armor made from inter-linked iron rings

**Mail-and-plate**
Mail armor to which solid metal plates were attached

**Musket**
A gun whose long barrel is smooth inside. It is usually loaded through the muzzle.

**Muzzle**
The open end of a gun barrel from which the bullet emerges

**Pan**
A cavity in a wheel lock, matchlock, and flintlock gun for gunpowder

**Phalanx**
A tight formation of foot soldiers usually carrying spears or pikes

**Pike**
A very long spear with a wooden shaft and a plain iron head

**Rifle**
A gun whose barrel has been cut with spiral grooves inside to make the bullet spin and so fly straighter

**Rivet**
A small metal pin with a flat head, hammered through holes in two overlapping metal plates. The other end is flattened to keep it in place.

**Scabbard**
A holder or sheath for a sword blade

**Scale**
A type of armor in which small plates, either of metal or some other material, are attached to a backing so they overlap downward

**Shell**
A metal projectile containing explosives, fired from a gun

**Shrapnel**
Fragments of an exploding projectile

**Slow match**
A glowing cord used to fire a matchlock. It was placed in the jaws of a metal holder called a serpent. When the trigger was pulled, it came down on gunpowder in a pan, which then set off the main charge.

**Submachine gun**
A portable automatic weapon that can be fired from the hip or shoulder

**Tiller**
The central wooden part of a crossbow

**Touchhole**
A small hole or vent in the top of a gun barrel through which the spark explodes the gunpowder inside

**Volley**
A discharge of many missiles at once

**Wad**
The paper holding the ball and powder in a gun barrel, often wrapped around them

**Winch**
A mechanism which fits over the end of the most powerful type of crossbow and uses pulleys to reduce the strength needed to wind back the cord

# ▶ Index